PEOPLE

EDL GO BOOK 1

PEOPLE

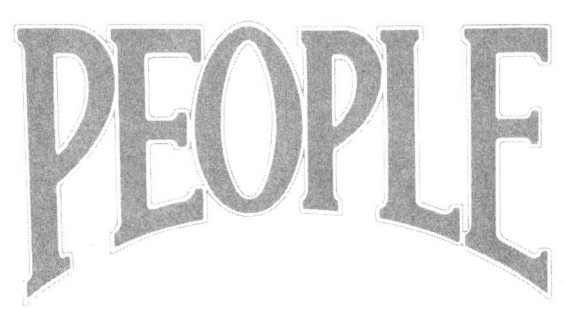

EDL GO Series Book 1

AUTHOR

Edith Goldstein

EDITORS

Estelle Kleinman

Daniel J. Domoff

ILLUSTRATORS

Anthony D'Adamo

Scott Nelson

ISBN 1-55855-661-3

Copyright © 1991, 1977 Steck-Vaughn Company. All rights reserved. No part of this book may be reproduced, or utilized in any form or by any means, electronic or mechanical, including photocopying, recording, or by any information storage and retrieval system, without permission in writing from the copyright owner. Requests for permission to make copies of any part of this book should be mailed to: Copyright Permissions, Steck-Vaughn Company, P.O. Box 26015, Austin, Texas 78755. Printed and bound in the United States.

13 14 15 16 RLB 00 99

CONTENTS

AA-1	The Cleaner	1
AA-2	Fired for Smoking	3
AA-3	What a Morning!	5
AA-4	Help for Two	7
AA-5	Jack Hits It Home	10
AA-6	Check that Story	12
AA-7	Help! Fire!	15
AA-8	That Mr. Bruno!	18
AA-9	Trouble Ride	21
AA-10	Pete Gets It Together	24
AA-11	Eve Gets Going	27
AA-12	What Good Are Taxes?	30
AA-13	Can Love Last?	33
AA-14	Two Weeks Together	36
AA-15	Don't Buy Trouble	39
AA-16	Two Loves	42
AA-17	That's My Job	45
AA-18	It's a Steal	48
AA-19	A Man Finds a Job	51
AA-20	The Gold Door	55
AA-21	Right On!	59
AA-22	Everything Happens to Mike	63
AA-23	The Crash	66
AA-24	The Tall Thin Man	70
AA-25	A Letter from Maria	74
AA-26	Make Up a Job	77
AA-27	One More Try	81
AA-28	Our Sun	85
AA-29	The American Cowboy	89
AA-30	Young Drinkers	93
Comprehension Questions		97
Answer Key		132

The Cleaner

Ken likes to show that he knows everything. Bob sees that it pays to let Ken show what he can do.

One ot the things I have to do at work is clean buses. Men, women, and children eat in the buses, and the buses look it when the day is over.

One day I was cleaning a bus, and Ken walked in. Ken knows everything, and he tells you that all the time. To Ken, the one way to do things is <u>his</u> way.

Ken said, "Bob, I'll show you the way to clean a bus with the cleaner <u>I</u> have." He went to work and I watched.

"That is a good cleaner you have. Where did you get it, Ken?" I asked.

Ken said, "I got it at the store for Janet. Janet likes to do all her work at home with it. What things do you want clean? Watch the way it works!"

I told Ken what I had to clean. He cleaned it and I watched. "You and that cleaner do a good job," I said.

Ken cleaned all day. All day I said over and over what a good cleaner he had and what good work he did.

That was a good day. The bus was cleaned. I didn't do the work. And I got the pay.

FIRED FOR SMOKING

Why fire a worker for smoking on the job? Bill learns why when he smokes at work.

Kay walked over to Bill and said, "Bill, you do not look good. What happened?"

"Kay, I got fired. That's what happened," said Bill.

Then Kay asked, "Didn't they like the way you work?"

"Yes, Kay, they liked the way I worked. That wasn't it," said Bill.

"Then why did they fire you?"

"I got fired for smoking on the job," said Bill.

"Look, Bill. Didn't they tell you about smoking when you started working? Didn't they tell you that all the workers have to go out the exits to smoke? Didn't you look about and see NO SMOKING everywhere?"

Then Bill said, "The exit is way over, Kay. I didn't want to walk all that way for a fast smoke. Not a thing happened when I smoked on the job. I ask you, can they fire workers for smoking?"

"Yes, they can," said Kay. "They know what can happen when someone smokes. They do not want workers put in the hospital. They know that fires can get started fast at jobs like the one you do. It happens every day. What about you, Bill? Do you want to put men and women in the hospital?"

"No, Kay. I do not want that. I have learned. I'll stop smoking." Then Bill said, "Kay, do you have one smoke for the last time?"

WHAT A MORNING!

Rosita works as a teller. One day something happened and Rosita had to work fast.

Rosita's job is cashing checks. One morning at work, Rosita happened to look and see 2 men. They looked at her and one of them said, "We want your cash. And we want it fast! Watch what you do. You will get it if you don't!"

Rosita didn't know what to do. Then she thought of something and said, "I don't have what you want. It's inside the safe. We will walk in and you can get all the cash you want."

The men thought that over and said, "OK." They walked to the safe with Rosita. Rosita thought, "When the men go inside the safe, I know something I can do to keep them in!"

When they all got inside, Rosita worked fast. Not one of them could get out!

Then Rosita said, "We are inside the safe and we can't get out without help. You know what will happen in time. We will go at one time. That will be it! Do you want that?"

The men thought it over and at last one said, "Do something! Time is going fast! We want out!"

"OK," said Rosita. "Put everything you have to one side. Then they will let you out."

A TV showed what was going on inside the safe. Men and women watched the 2 men do what Rosita wanted. Then they let them out.

They got the 2 men! And Rosita was OK!

All Rosita said was, "What a morning! I have all my work to do and it's time to eat."

That Rosita is something!

HELP FOR TWO

Linda Chan liked George Wah, and she liked to help him. What would she do when he was gone?

Many days, Linda Chan didn't like her job at the hospital. On days like that, she wanted to stop working. Then George Wah got put into the hospital, and, in time, Linda learned something.

One day when Linda was helping George out of bed, he said, "In the morning, I'll tell you a story about some parents who had to help some children when they got into a fight. You'll like the story. It will be fun for you."

"I will stop for the story if I have time," Linda told him.

In the morning, George waited and waited for Linda. She'll have time, he thought.

Linda had many things to do that morning. When all her work was out of the way, she went to see George.

"I was waiting to get together with you," he said.

Then George told his story. He had a good way of telling a story, and Linda liked it. "It was a good story," she said.

"Linda," George said when she started to go, "I will show you something about baseball in the morning."

Linda looked at George. "What?" she asked.

"I will tell you a story about hitting," he said. "I can hit a baseball. When I get out, I may play again. In the morning, I'll have a good story for you."

"You can't walk," Linda said. "Why talk about playing again?"

"With your help, I'll do it," George said.

"I'll see about helping," Linda said.

In the morning, Linda talked to the doctor. He told her she could help, and he told her what to do.

In time, George did walk out of the hospital. Linda watched George go and thought about her job — the job she had learned to like when she was helping George.

Jack hits it home

Baseball players like to make home runs. But this was one home run Jack <u>didn't</u> like.

Jack was happy about his window. He had worked and waited to get it and to pay for it. He liked what it did for his home. He liked the way the window looked from the outside, and he liked to look out from the inside.

But one day he looked out and he could see men playing ball in the lot.

Jack wasn't happy to see that. He thought that some day that ball could break his window. What could he do?

Jack went over and talked to the men. "Don't hit the ball over that way, men. Someone will break the window I put in."

The men looked at the window. "That is a good job you did," one of them said. "No one wants to break it and have to pay for it."

"That's good. I had to pay a lot for it," Jack said.

They went on talking, and the men asked Jack to play ball with them. He liked that.

They played ball every night. Jack played, but he watched when they started to hit the ball. "Watch it! Don't forget that window," he said over and over.

One night they played the Cash Cleaners. The men said, "OK, Jack. It's 3 to 3, and it's all yours. You can do it!"

"Watch me," Jack said. It was a fast ball and a good hit.

"It's a home run! A home run! You did it, Jack," the men said.

But Jack didn't run. He couldn't run. He watched the ball. He watched the ball hit and break his window!

CHECK THAT STORY

Why was Tony running? Jim put 2 and 2 together, but he didn't get 4.

Jim started to walk to work one morning. On the way, he met Angela. Angela asked, "Jim, did you see what was going on this morning? All I could see was Tony. He was outside running in the street. Is he in trouble?"

"Not that I know, Angela. I don't know one thing about it," said Jim.

Angela went on, and Jim thought about what she had said. Then he met Ed. Jim asked Ed, "Do you know what happened? Why was Tony running in the street?"

Ed said, "They say some man was breaking into the drugstore Do you think it was Tony? I did see a policeman going after some man."

Then Jim said, "I'll bet Tony is on drugs."

With that, Jim went into Goodman's Store and said to the storekeeper, "Do you know what? Tony is on drugs and he was breaking into the drugstore this morning. A policeman got Tony out on the street."

The storekeeper said, "What a thing to happen! My, my, I don't know what to think."

Then Doctor Clayton walked in. Jim told the doctor about Tony.

Doctor Clayton looked like he was going to have a fit! Then he said, "This is some story you are giving me! Let me tell you something. Tony is NOT in trouble! He is NOT on drugs! And he did NOT break into the drugstore! Yes, he was running in the street this morning. He was running to get the bus. Where did you get this story?"

Jim did not look happy. Then he said, "It looks like I did it again. I put things together without thinking. And I didn't check one thing. What can I say? I will not do it again."

AA-7

HELP! FIRE!

Ed and Mary Kennan are good friends to have when you are in trouble. Dan Goodson and his father find this out when the Goodsons' home is on fire.

Ed and Mary Kennan walked home from work together. "That's where Dan Goodson and his father live now, over the drugstore," Ed said.

"But they loved the home they had," Mary said. "Why didn't they keep it?"

"They wanted to keep it, but couldn't," Ed told her. "Just when Dan's father, Mr. Goodson, got a job he liked, a bus hit him. The doctors said that he'll never walk again. And he can't work at all now. Some people just never get the breaks."

"Look at that window!" Mary said.

Ed looked. He could see smoke inside.

"The Goodsons' home is on fire!" said Mary.

"Get the fire fighters," Ed said. "I'll go inside and see if I can help Dan get his father out."

"Watch out, Ed," Mary was telling him. "If the fire gets to you—" But Ed had run inside and didn't know Mary was saying something to him.

Inside, there was smoke and fire all over. It was some job, but Ed and Dan got Mr. Goodson out on the sidewalk fast. They sat on the sidewalk with him, and they looked beat! Mary sat with them.

It was some fire, and many people watched what was going on. Then the fire fighters got there. They went to work and put out the fire. When it was just about over, one of the people watching said, "Look! They are going to be on TV!"

The TV people walked over to Mr. Goodson and asked him, "With all that smoke and fire, did you think you could get out in time?"

"No," said Mr. Goodson. "I thought this was my last night to live. But then Ed Kennan and my son Dan got me out."

"It was some job," Dan told them. "I could never have lasted without Ed's help."

Then the TV people asked Ed, "Why did you go into all that smoke and fire? It wasn't safe at all."

"I didn't stop to think about it," Ed said. "Someone had to help out, and so I did."

She: "Baseball, baseball. That's all you think about. I bet you can't tell me the day we met."
He: "Oh, but I can! It was the day I hit 2 home runs!"

THAT MR. BRUNO!

What is it like not to see?
Mr. Bruno never lets it stop him.

That's Mr. Bruno's store over there on the corner. You can buy just about everything in it. Lots of people go in to buy things. Mr. Bruno helps them all find what they want.

But do you know something? Mr. Bruno can't see! He never could see a thing, but he didn't give in. He can do many of the things that you and I can do. But how can he do them if he can't see? I'll never know.

Mr. Bruno has help in his store. Jill Farmer works for him every morning. And Mike Day works after school. So they can do the things that Mr. Bruno can't. But Mr. Bruno knows where everything is in the store. And he knows everything that goes on inside and outside of his store.

I'll tell you about some of the things he can do. Then you'll see what kind of man he is.

For one thing, Mr. Bruno can help people buy the books in his store. They tell him the ones they want and he goes and finds the books for them. He can't see to read, but he gets the books they want every time!

Children go in to Mr. Bruno's store every day. Sometimes they will not have a cent with them, and they'll want something that they can't pay for. They'll start walking out with a book or something like that.

Somehow Mr. Bruno has a way of knowing when this happens. He'll tell them, "Now, I want you to put that over there where you got it. That way of doing things is no good. It will get you in trouble."

That tells you something about Mr. Bruno. You can see what kind of man he is.

Let me tell you what happened with my friend Julio.

One day Julio came in to the store and Mr. Bruno said, "Why aren't you happy today, Julio? Did something happen with you and Maria last night? Did you have a fight?"

Now, how did Mr. Bruno know about that? That Mr. Bruno! He can't see, but he knows a lot about everything. Who knows? Maybe he can see things with his mind!

Trouble Ride

A bus ride isn't always a time to make new friends.

"Are you going to LA?" I asked.

The boy was looking out the window. I started to ask again, but something told me not to. He wasn't lost, and he didn't have to talk. I had a good job waiting for me in LA. All I had to do was keep out of trouble.

After some time, the boy looked at me and said, "What is the name of this station?"

"I think it is named Barstow," I told him.

The bus started out again on the last hours of the ride. The boy looked out the window again, and I looked the other way. He was going to LA or near it, but that wasn't something I had to know.

After a little time, the boy said, "There may be trouble in LA. That man who got on in Barstow is after me."

I didn't want to know a thing, but I couldn't tell him that. "Why?" I asked.

The boy didn't like his parents. He said they hit him a lot. He was on his way to see friends. They had said he could live with them. "That man who got on is a policeman," the boy said. "I know him, but he doesn't know me. I think he will try to stop me in LA. If you tell him that you and I are together, he will go on his way. Can you do that? Can you give me a break?"

I didn't want any trouble, but how could I walk out on the boy? I couldn't just forget the way he looked when he said his parents hit him. He didn't like them at all. Going home wasn't going to help him.

"I'll help," I said, "but after that, you go on your way."

When the bus got to LA, I learned the man was a policeman, and he was after the boy. My trouble started when I said the boy was with me.

Now I have to talk my way out of this thing. I don't know if the boy's parents hit him, but I do know one thing he forgot to tell me. He didn't say a thing about poisoning them.

PETE GETS IT TOGETHER

Pete didn't talk a lot. Then one day he met someone he wanted to talk to.

It was a bad time for Pete. He was getting taller and taller, and he was falling over things all the time. Pete never did one thing right. He just couldn't get it all together.

Pete didn't have many friends. He never could think of things to talk about. And he was no good at baseball. Every time Pete wanted to play, the other boys said, "Get lost. We don't want you. You're no good to us."

Pete's parents thought he was OK. He didn't talk a lot, but that was all right with them. They had 3 girls and they all talked together all the time. So Pete could not break in when he did want to talk.

Pete didn't like girls. When the girls at home had girl friends over, Pete liked to keep out of the way.

One day Pete was on his way home from school. He wasn't looking where he was going and walked right into a garbage can. Over it went. Garbage all over the street! Pete looked at it and thought, "So what!"

Then he thought, "Rats go for garbage. I've got to get rid of this. Better clean the street."

Pete started to put the garbage into the can again.

"Look at me," he thought. "If someone I know comes this way and sees me, I'll want to hide out for days."

Pete covered the can and started walking again. But just then, Sue walked out of her home. Pete and Sue went to school together, but they had never talked.

Sue said, "I watched you put that garbage into the can. Not many people think about things like that."

"It was nothing," Pete said with a funny look. "I was happy to do it. I like clean streets."

"So do other people," said Sue. "But you did something about it!"

The day after this, Sue came over to Pete in school. The school day was just about over. "How are you today?" she asked.

"OK!" said Pete. "And you?"

"Not bad. Not bad at all." Then Sue said, "Walking home?"

Pete said, "Yes."

"If you're going my way," said Sue, "why don't we walk together?"

Pete was so happy he couldn't talk. But Sue didn't mind. She liked it that Pete didn't talk a lot.

Now, Pete and Sue see a lot of one another. Pete thinks he's getting it together now. Maybe he is. He isn't falling over things all the time now. He's just falling in love.

Eve Gets Going

What can you do when you have lost your job? Eve thinks of something.

Just as the fall started, Eve lost her job.

The store she worked in wasn't doing so hot. It couldn't keep so many workers. So Eve was "let go."

Eve was mad. "You can be out of a job in no time at all," she said to a friend at the store. "It's not right." Then Eve got her things together and went home.

On her way home, she thought, "What can I do?" She wasn't mad now, just sad and tired. She didn't walk fast. She was lost in her thoughts.

Eve came to the boarding house where she lived. "How will I live?" she thought. "How will I pay my rent? I don't know if I can find another job in this city."

Just then, another thought came into Eve's mind, like a ray of light. "Why this city?" she thought. "I don't have to live here at all!" Eve ran into the house. She wanted to do some thinking.

After one hour, Eve came out of the house. She went over to see Mrs. Cook, the landlady.

"Yes, Eve?" said Mrs. Cook. "How are you? What can I do for you?"

"Mrs. Cook," Eve said, "I have lost my job."

"Eve! How sad! What will you do?"

"I'm not sad, Mrs. Cook. I'm happy!"

"What are you saying, Eve?" said Mrs. Cook. "I don't get it."

"I'm going," Eve said. "Here is my last rent."

"But where will you go? What will you do?"

"I don't know," said Eve. "Another city, maybe. I just don't know. But I'll think of something. I have my health. I'll be OK."

Mrs. Cook said, "But Eve, you can't go. Not just like that!"

"Why not?" said Eve. "I have no job. Nothing is keeping me here. No one tells me that I must live here. I'll find something, somewhere."

Mrs. Cook said nothing. Eve started to go, but then she looked at Mrs. Cook again.

"Sometimes," said Eve, "you just have to do what you want to do. Many people do just what others tell them to do. I don't want to live like that."

Eve started to go again, and she thought, "I know that a lot of good things are out there waiting for me. All I have to do is find them!"

What Good Are TAXES?

Why do we have to spend all that money on taxes? Pat tells Ramon where all the money goes.

"Pat, will you help me out?" asked Ramon.

"OK, Ramon, what is it?"

"Well, Pat, when I came to this land, I didn't know a lot about the ways of your people. I have learned some, but not all."

"What can I help you with, Ramon?"

"What can you tell me about taxes?" asked Ramon.

"What can I tell you about taxes? That's a good one! I pay taxes all the time and so do you. Taxes are money everyone has to pay, one way or the other. I have to pay taxes on the money I get from work. A lot of the tax money is out of my paycheck when I get it.

"Then there are taxes on many of the things we buy in stores. And people pay taxes on the houses they live in."

"But, Pat, I don't have a house. I pay rent. Do I get out of paying that tax?"

"No, Ramon, you don't. Your landlord has to pay that tax, and some of your rent money goes to pay for it."

"Say, Pat, what happens to all the tax money?"

"Ramon, the money goes for many things. Some goes to the city. The city pays the fire fighters, the garbage workers, and the police with tax money."

"Tell me, Pat, does tax money pay for schools too?"

"Yes, tax money pays for new schools and for keeping up the ones that are not new. It pays your teachers and all the other people that work in the schools."

"What other things does tax money pay for?"

"Let's see now. Some pays for our streets and some pays for the people who work on them and keep them clean. Taxes pay the people working at the Board of Health and at the hospitals too. And more tax money pays for things like the lot you play ball in. Then, too, it pays for some of the shows you see. The city spends a lot of our tax money to let us have some fun and good times."

"It looks like we get a lot for our taxes, Pat."

"Yes, it's not too good to pay a lot of money in taxes, but then think of some of the things we get for it. Then you can see why we have to pay taxes."

"Say, Pat, you're a good teacher. I got a lot from your talk about taxes."

CAN LOVE LAST?

Being in school isn't for James when he's in love with Alice.

But is it good to get out?

Alice was walking out of school one day with James when he said, "School, school, school! That's all you think about and that's all you talk about. What about us?"

"Look, James," said Alice. "I love you and you know I think about us a lot. But we are in school and we have to think about that too."

Then James said, "School isn't where it's at. School is for children, and I'm getting out fast. I'll get a job and somewhere to live."

"But, James, think how much money you'll need for that. You'll have to eat and pay rent. And you'll need money for a lot of other things. And how can you get a job? The teachers and the TV ads all say you've got to have schooling to get a job that pays good money. You could be in for a lot of trouble if you walk out of school now."

"That's what you think, Alice. You just watch me. I'll show you. When I get things together, you'll see that my plan is OK. It worked for Joe. He got out of school and got a job. He and Sally are together and they are happy."

"That's what you think, James. I saw Sally last week. She told me Joe went away without her. He had a job, but he didn't get much pay. No schooling, no money, that's what he told her. Then the bills started coming in and they hadn't saved a penny. They couldn't pay their bills. Love went right out the window for them. Please, James, think things over."

"Look, Alice, I'm not Joe, so forget him. I'll give some thought to what you said. Some of the things you say are OK. But I don't know. I don't look at most things the way you do. I have to do what's going to be right for me."

"You do that," Alice said, "and I'll do what's right for me."

Ben: "Do you think a lot of people read the Want Ads?"
Len: "I *know* they do. Last week I put in an ad for a night watchman, and that night we were robbed!"

AA-14

TWO WEEKS TOGETHER

Two weeks with no work <u>and</u> a paycheck. How will the Ortegas and the Bensons spend that time?

June and Ed Benson and Maria and Pedro Ortega are good friends. June and Maria spend a lot of time together and Pedro and Ed work together.

One night Ed told June, "Pedro and I will not be working for two weeks. It could be fun if we all went somewhere together for the two weeks."

June said, "That's for me, all right! I bet the Ortegas will like it too. Let's get them over to talk about it."

June talked to the Ortegas, and they stopped in after supper.

"Come on in and let me have your coats," said June. "Ed was getting cleaned up after his class, but here he is now."

Maria asked, "Where do you want to go, Ed? Somewhere hot? Somewhere cold?"

"Wait up," said Pedro. "If we are going somewhere, we have to plan. How much money can we get together? If we know that, we will know how much we can spend and what we can do."

"You're right," said June. "Somewhere cold could be fun, but we may need to get a lot of new clothes. Maybe somewhere hot is better. We will not need so many things."

"Yes," said Maria. "Let's go where it's hot. I can just see us all having a good time on the sand."

"Say, I've been thinking," said Pedro. "There are enough fun things we could do right here. We don't need to go somewhere to have fun."

"You're right," said June. "And that way we don't need to spend money getting somewhere. We could spend it all on fun things here."

"Maybe you're right," said Joe. "We could have some cookouts, go to some shows, hear the band at the park, and go to some ball games."

Pedro went on to say, "I think this is good planning, because it's better if we don't spend all our money. It could pay us all if we save some. There could be a time when things are not so good at work. We could need our savings then. And I think we could have a good time right here at home. What do you say, Maria?"

"I don't know," said Maria. "I was kind of planning on going somewhere for a little time. I just

37

wanted to see something new. Couldn't we? Please?"

June, Ed, and Pedro all thought a little. Then June said, "OK, how about this? We have two weeks. Why not one week at home and the other week we'll go somewhere? What do you all think?"

"But what about all that talk about saving money?" said Pedro.

"One week will not be a lot of money," said Ed. "I think it's OK."

"OK, Maria," said Pedro. "We'll do it."

"That's what I wanted to hear!" said Maria. "Now, where will we go? Somewhere hot? Or somewhere cold?"

Don't Buy Trouble

**Sometimes a "bargain" can cost a lot.
Read this newspaper story to find out why.**

A fast-talking salesman has been putting one over on men and women in Newton for the last two weeks.

His way of getting cash away from people came to light when the police called this paper and asked us to run a story on the man they call the "bargain" salesman.

At 11:30 this morning, Will Walker, 25, of Sand Street, came to Police Station #122 to ask for help.

Walker said he had been looking at the coats in the window of Bellson's Men's Store. He was standing near Bellson's sign when a man came over and started talking to him. The two men talked a little about baseball and then Walker happened to say he was going to buy a coat. Walker showed the man a coat in the window that he liked, but Walker said he thought it cost too much.

Then the man told Walker that he was selling the same coat, but not for so much money. He said he sold clothes house-to-house and that his things are bargains.

He said if Walker could give him $30.00, he could get the coat Walker wanted in one hour.

Walker first started to give the man a check, but the man said he had to have cash. So Walker came up with the cash.

Walker stayed outside Bellson's for two hours, but the man never came with the coat, or with Walker's cash!

Walker then went to the police and asked them to find the "bargain" salesman and get his money for him.

Police say this is not the first time someone has been cleaned out by this salesman. It's happened to ten other people over the last two weeks.

Police say the "bargain" salesman is about 35, tall, good-looking, and fast-talking.

If you see or meet this man, call the police or this paper and tell what you know. Your call may be the one that stops him.

Pete forgot things all the time. He went to his girl friend's house one day and said, "I know I forget things. I forget everything that's said to me. Now I *know* that I asked you to be my Mrs. last night, but I forgot what you said."

She looked at him and said, "It's good that you came over. I know that I said no to someone, but I forgot it was you."

TWO LOVES

A new car and a girl friend who wants to learn to drive it! How can Tim Buyer get out of this one?

Tim Buyer never thought he could ever get a car like the one he just got. What a good-looking car it is! And Tim wants to keep it looking that way. Every time he gets home from driving it, he cleans the inside. Then he gets water and cleans the outside.

Tim wants to keep his car looking new, so he will not drive it to work. He rides the bus every day.

Tim says, "I want to be on the safe side. I don't want something to happen to my car in the lot at work. That lot is bad news for a new car."

Tim's girl friend Sue is happy about the car too. Now that Tim has a car, she wants to learn to drive. Then, when Tim goes to work, she can have the car all day. That is, if she learns to drive. Sue hasn't told

Tim about this, but he knows she's thinking about learning to drive his car.

Tim and Sue are in love, she has his ring, and they have never had a bad fight. But it looks like they may be in for a bad time because of the car. When Tim thinks about Sue learning to drive in his car, he just gets sick!

Sue knows Tim is not happy about letting her learn to drive in his car. So she isn't saying a thing about it. And Tim isn't saying a thing about it to her. You could say they have a lot on their minds they're not talking about.

One night Sue asked Tim over for supper. She cooked all day, and it was some supper. But they didn't talk much. Then Tim looked up and said,

"Sue, I think it's time you hurried up and learned to drive."

Sue thought she wasn't hearing right. "You what?" she said.

So Tim said it again. "It's time you learned to drive. After all, you could drive my car."

Tim went on, "Sue, I saw an ad in tonight's paper. A driving class is starting a week from today. I want you to go, and I'll pay for it because I want you to have a good teacher. Besides, that way you'll learn on the teacher's car, not on my car. When you're a good driver, you can drive my car."

Sue was happy to hear Tim say this. She said, "Tim! Let's go for a ride in your car!"

"OK," said Tim. "I'll drive you wherever you want to go."

"Good," Sue said, "and some day, I'll drive you!"

If your son wants to learn to drive, don't stand in his way.

That's My Job

**It's a lot of walking,
but this mailman
likes his job.**

Here it is Monday morning again. No day is longer than Monday. More mail comes on Monday than all the other days in the week.

Good thing I like my job and I like to walk. All this walking, day after day, could get to you. Being a mailman has its ups and downs—like up one side of the street and down the other!

But this job gives me time to get to know people and to do a lot of thinking. And it's fun to talk with the people I meet. You can make a lot of new friends when you're a mailman.

Let's see, the first house is Mrs. Mano's. She's been waiting for a letter from her son. He works and goes to school over in New City. Mrs. Mano sat at her window all last week waiting for me. "Mrs. Mano? Are you home?"

"Good morning, Sam. How are you today?"

"OK, Mrs. Mano. Say, I haven't got a letter from your son. Is everything OK?"

"Yes it is, Sam. I talked to him the other day. He says he'll write me a letter in a week or so. He hasn't got much time for writing."

"I know. He's got a lot to do. OK, Mrs. Mano. I've got to be going."

"See you, Sam."

Look at this. More bills for Mr. Sellers. He just gets bills and no letters. "Good morning, Mr. Sellers. How are you today?"

"It's you again! With more bills for me, right? I'll bet you just love to give me my bills."

"Wait up, Mr. Sellers. Don't start fighting with me. It's my job to give you your mail. If you get a lot of bills, that's your trouble. So don't get mad at me."

"The bills are going right in the garbage!"

"Have a good day, Mr. Sellers!" That got him!

Look, there's June Story waiting for me. Her boyfriend writes every day. "Good morning, June!"

"Sam! Is there a letter for me?"

"Yes, there is. Say, when is your boyfriend getting home again?"

"Two weeks, Sam."

"That's good. Not as much mail for me to give out! See you in the morning."

Well, on to the other houses. It's a good thing the weekly ads aren't in today's mail. Monday is bad enough without them. Like I say, being a mailman has its ups and downs, but that's my job and I like it.

It's a Steal

"Shopping" without paying costs everyone a lot in the long run.

Do you ever wonder why things in stores cost so much? Most of us know some of the things that make costs go up. But there is one thing that we don't think about much.

Every day people steal things from stores. People steal food, clothes, books, or anything! It can happen at any store. It may be in the best store in the city. It happens in big stores and little stores. And who pays for the things that people steal? We all do, because the cost of everything must go up when people steal.

Who are the people who steal from stores? You may think that it's just people who have no money. But this is not so. One newspaper says that nearly all the people who steal have the money to pay. Sometimes people with a lot of money have been stopped by store police. They don't need what they steal. They may steal "for fun." They may steal just to see if they can get out of the store without paying.

Some people think that just children steal from stores, or just people up to 20. But again, this isn't so. Children do steal from stores, but so do people right up to 80 and over!

A newspaper says that one buyer out of every 15 steals. You can see that this runs into a lot of money. And it's not just "buyers" who steal. Sometimes, the workers or the salespeople may steal too! They steal right out of the store they work for. It goes on all the time.

What happens when a store finds someone who is stealing something? You may think that a store may let someone go the first time he or she steals. At one time, stores did this. They let the stealer go, and then they watched the stealer closely the next time he or she came into the store. But stores don't do this any more. Here's what happens now:

If the store gets the stealer in the store, they call the police and hand over the one who is stealing. If the stealer has left the store, the police go right after her or him.

A store will call the police if someone is stealing something that costs as little as 25 cents! This is because stores want to put a stop to all stealing. To do this, the stores must go after everyone who steals.

If a stealer wants to fix things up, the store won't let him or her do it. The stealer may say, "I'll pay for it now!" Or the stealer may say, "I give you my word. I will not steal again." But that's not good enough. Stealing makes all our costs go up. If stores call the police every time someone steals, then maybe, just maybe, the stealing will stop.

Don: "What time is it?"
Lon: "It's two o'clock."
Don: "How about that! I've been asking people all day, and everyone gives me some other time."

A MAN FINDS A JOB

**Are you a boy or a man at 18?
Rusty shows that he is a man.**

When Rusty was 18, he got out of school. He went looking for a job, but he couldn't find one. Not at first, anyway. He walked up and down all the streets, looking for work. Every day he checked the newspaper. There was nothing.

One store had a sign in the window. It said, "Help Wanted." Rusty went inside. The man who ran the store needed a salesman. He said to Rusty, "You're only 18? Forget it! I need a man for this job, not a boy!"

Rusty was mad. He thought, "Maybe I would not be a good salesman, but he has no right to call me a boy!"

One day Rusty happened to hear that Chuck's Corner Station needed help. They needed someone to work on cars. Rusty loved cars and he loved to work on them. "I'll go over to Chuck's to see if I can get that job." And so he went.

Rusty pushed the door and went inside. He stopped in the middle of the room. Chuck was eating, so he didn't see Rusty at first. At last, Chuck looked up. "Yes?" Chuck said.

"I fix cars," Rusty said.

"So? So do I," said Chuck.

"I hear you need someone new," said Rusty.

"I get it," Chuck said. "You want a job. Yes, we're looking for someone. Let's see what you can do."

Chuck showed Rusty a car. "Let's take this car out for a ride. You drive. I want you to tell me if it needs fixing. And I want you to tell me just what it needs."

They got in. Rusty started the car and pulled out into the street. As he was driving away from the station, Rusty said, "This car is moving like a truck. Something's not right. I think I know what it is."

Rusty went up and down the street two more times. Then he came back into the station. He looked at Chuck and said, "I think the trouble is in the 'drive.' I can fix it, but it will take a lot of work."

"OK," said Chuck. "Let's do it."

Rusty worked for hours and Chuck worked with him. Together, they fixed the car. Chuck looked over Rusty's work. "Good work!" said Chuck. "The job is yours!" Rusty was too tired to say how happy he was.

Just then, a man came into the station. It was the man who had called Rusty "a boy"! The man said to Chuck, "Is my car fixed?"

"Yes, it is," said Chuck. "All fixed. Rusty just did a good job on it."

The man looked at Rusty. He said, "Don't I know you? Have I ever met you anywhere?"

Rusty looked at him and said, "No. I don't think so."

Then the man said, "Well, anyway, Chuck must be happy to have a good man like you working for him."

Now why do you think Rusty thought that was funny?

One way to be a better driver is to have a policeman driving in the car next to you.

Jack: "What's the best thing to take when you are run down?"
Mack: "The driver's name."

THE GOLD DOOR *

Why did the storyteller get the paper that said, "The Gold Door"? What would happen when he opened "The Gold Door"?

Many days I like to walk and look in all the shop windows. One hot day as I was window shopping, I saw an old man standing on the street, handing out little papers. I thought that it must be an ad for one of the stores. I walked over and got a paper from the man. All it said was: "The Gold Door."

I didn't know of a shop nearby with that name. Maybe it was a new place. I didn't think about it much. I was about to walk away when I saw the man give one of the papers to a girl. The girl looked at the paper, read it, and left it on the street. I know that the shopkeepers had a hard time keeping the streets clean, so I went to get the paper. The words on the paper read: "Eat at Joe's."

*Note: This story is based on a story by O. Henry.

I thought it was funny that the girl's paper said "Eat at Joe's" when my paper said "The Gold Door." I walked over to the old man and got a new paper. Again it said "The Gold Door." At the same time the old man gave a paper to a boy. I looked at his paper. It said: "Eat at Joe's."

"There must be something important about my paper," I thought. "I must find out what 'The Gold Door' is."

Before I had time to do any more thinking, I saw that the old man was standing next to a big house. Many people lived inside. Maybe I would find out about "The Gold Door" in there. Something made me run in. Yes, there it was, way up the steps—a gold door!

I ran up the steps and I pushed on the bell. But no one came. The door was open, so I went in. There was a girl standing on a box, and she was about to jump out the window! I ran over and stopped her just in time. I pulled her away from the window.

She was a lovely girl, but she had sad, sad eyes. She told me all of her troubles. "Things haven't been easy for me," she said. "I have no money, and I've just lost my job. I have never been so sad."

I said, "Isn't there anyone to help you?"

"No. No one."

I looked at her closely. "I can help you," I said. "Do you want me to?"

She looked into my eyes. "Yes," she said. "Please help me." Her eyes looked better now. Not so sad—maybe a little happy!

"Let's go get something to eat," I said. "We'll talk all about your troubles."

We went out. I closed the gold door, and we went down the steps hand in hand. That's when I saw something funny! All the other doors in the house were gold too!

So why had I run up to her door?

On the street the old man was handing out his papers. I walked over to him.

"Let me ask you something," I said. "Why did you hand me two papers that said 'The Gold Door'?

57

All the other people got papers that said 'Eat at Joe's.'"

The old man looked up. "Oh, did you get all the papers with 'The Gold Door' on them? You see, I work for Joe, and he pays me to hand out papers saying 'Eat at Joe's.' But my friend is going to be in a new play that's opening on Monday. She asked me to hand out some ads for that play. See, it's opening over there."

I looked to the other side of the street. There was a big sign there. It said, "Opening Monday—'The Gold Door.'"

I looked at the girl walking next to me. She looked happy. She said, "Isn't it funny, how things happen in our lives?"

"Yes, it is," I said. "Yes, it is."

I'm Here

Look at me, see me,
Know that I'm here.
Talk to me. Walk with me.
Know when I'm near.
Say what you want to me,
Fight with me, play,
But when I look right at you,
Don't look the other way.

RIGHT ON!

**What can you do
if you don't like things the way they are?
June and Ann know what to do.**

"It just makes me so mad," June said to Ann. "It's the only food store that's near enough for us to walk to. And everything about it is so bad!"

"I know," said Ann. "Food costs more there than in the other stores in the city. And most of it isn't very good. The meat is nothing but fat. They don't keep foods cold enough, and some boxes of food are all wet."

June went on. "I've talked to the storekeeper about all the things that are wrong. But he hasn't fixed anything. Things are no better!"

"Well, it's time to do something," Ann said. "We're sick and tired of being ripped off every time we shop in that store. Let's think of something."

"Right on!" said June.

So June and Ann worked out a plan. Then they told 20 friends about it. The plan was to let dollars talk to the storekeeper.

Everyone knows that stores make money on what shoppers spend. If a shopper spends as little as ten dollars, some of this is money in the bank for the storekeeper.

If one or two shoppers stop spending their money in the store, the storekeeper may not miss it. But, if enough shoppers stop shopping in the store, the storekeeper will miss it. Then he will have to do something to bring the shoppers in again. A store is there to make money, and it cannot keep running without a lot of shoppers.

This was the plan that Ann and June had:

First, they and the 20 other shoppers got together to make signs. The signs were big enough to catch everyone's eye, and they said things like: STAND UP FOR YOUR RIGHTS! THIS STORE IS A RIP-OFF! BE SMART AND DON'T SHOP HERE! WE WANT MORE FOR OUR MONEY!

When they had enough signs, the shoppers started to walk up and down the street by the store. They walked all around the store with the signs. People who were going in to shop saw them and stopped to read the signs. Most of them did not go in to shop.

Before long, the newspaper learned what was

going on and sent someone over to talk to June and Ann. When the story hit the paper, most people stopped shopping in the store.

Then, the storekeeper slipped out and called the women in for a talk. They had him now!

He said if they would start shopping in the store again, he would get good meat and better things for them to buy. He would keep the costs the same as other stores in the city. And he would keep the store clean.

The women liked what he had to say. They would get what they wanted. They would have a better store to shop in and their dollars would buy more and better things.

When a lot of people get together, they can do things that one or two cannot. June and Ann learned that people have a much better chance of righting a wrong when they all work together.

Can It Be?

Whenever I go somewhere at night
The others have clothes that look just right.
They all know what to do and say.
How do they ever get that way?

Tonight Joe said, "Just look at you.
You know all the right things to do."
And then I thought, "Can it be
They think that, when they look at me?"

Everything Happens to Mike

**Why was Mike having all those accidents?
Gus finds out why.**

Things happened to Mike all the time. Every time he ran into Gus, Mike had a new story to tell. But not one of them was good.

Mike said, "Gus, everything happens to me. I don't know what's going on with me. I just have one accident after another. In the last two weeks, I've had five falls. I've been at the hospital so many times, everyone there knows me."

Gus didn't like to see his friend having so many troubles, and he wanted to help.

"Look, Mike, tell me all about it. Maybe I can help. How do these accidents happen? Maybe there's something that makes them happen."

"I don't know what it is about me, Gus. Sometimes I think accidents just wait for me to come by. Like the other day . . . I was just going into the cleaners. I pushed open the door and down I went. How was I to know they were doing the place over? I was out cold for an hour. When I came to, I was at the hospital . . . and the doctor was fixing up my hand."

"But Mike, wasn't there a 'Danger' sign?" asked Gus.

"I don't know. Maybe there was, maybe there wasn't. If there was, I didn't see it. You know me, I must have been thinking about something important and wasn't looking where I was going."

"But Mike, you've got to watch where you're going. Thinking doesn't do you any good when you get hurt and have to go to the hospital. I tell you what. Let's go get something to eat and talk some more. I just thought of something. If I'm right, maybe things will get better for you."

Mike and Gus walked down the street. All at once, Gus said, "Mike, look at the big sign on that place. How can they get away with putting THAT on a sign?"

"I see the sign, Gus, but I can't make out what it says. I'll have to get right up to it to read what it says."

"I've got it! I've got it! Mike, now I know why you have so many accidents. You don't see well. You've got to see an eye doctor. A doctor can fix you up so you can see to read signs. Let's telephone a doctor right away."

The next day, Gus drove Mike to see the eye doctor. When Mike came out, he said, "Gus, it pays to have a friend like you. I don't know how I got by before I went to the eye doctor. I couldn't see those safety lines on the street, I couldn't read signs, and I couldn't see anything that wasn't right up close to me. The doctor said it was a wonder that I haven't had an accident that finished me off. But he gave me these and now I can see just as well as anyone. Say, how about going back and taking a look at that sign you showed me. I never did find out what it said!"

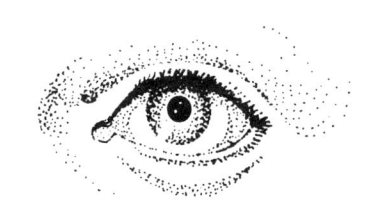

THE CRASH

It's important to help when there's an accident. But it's just as important to know the right things to do.

It was the middle of the night and most people were sleeping. Jan Coats was walking home. She started across the street. Just as she got to the middle, a car came out of nowhere . . . going fast! Jan jumped out of its way and it just missed hitting her.

The car ripped on down the street. Then, CRASH! It hit another car!

Everything was quiet again. Too quiet!

Jan ran down to the two cars and looked in. She didn't hear a thing. She didn't see anyone move. Were they living? Jan couldn't tell. But she could tell that it was up to her to get help.

She ran to a nearby house and started ringing the bell as hard as she could. Nothing happened, so she called out, "Help! Help! I need help!"

At last a man came to the door. He was having a hard time keeping his eyes open. "What's going on? What do you want at this time of night?"

"There's been a bad accident down the street," said Jan. "Some people are badly hurt. We can't just leave them there. Call the police and tell them to hurry!"

"OK," said the man. "I am going to get some clothes on. I'll be ready right away!"

"Hurry," said Jan. "They can't last long without help."

In no time, Jan and the man were at the cars.

"Let's get them out," said the man.

"No," said Jan. "You have to know how to move people who are hurt. We'd better wait for the police."

"OK, but let's try to get the doors open. That will save the police some time."

They got one car open with no trouble. The other was a hard job, but they worked together and got it open at last.

A police car pulled up. One policeman said, "The doctors are on the way. It's a good thing you called so fast. And it's good you got the car doors open. Fast work can save lives."

Just then, the doctors got there. They got the people out of the cars and started to work on them.

One of the doctors looked up at Jan and said, "Your smart thinking may have saved the two drivers. It's good that you didn't move them. You have to know just what to do with someone who has been badly hurt. Moving people who are hurt like this can hurt them more than it helps."

One of the policemen asked Jan about the accident. Jan told him, "I don't know how it happened. One car was going very fast. I was trying to get across the street and it nearly hit me. It looked like the driver never saw the other car. It's not easy to see at night."

The policeman said, "That's not it! I could see all right. They must have been driving so fast that they couldn't stop in time. Driving too fast doesn't pay."

Jan Coats said quietly, "The two drivers paid a lot tonight. Maybe too much."

Tom: "It's a good thing you named me Tom."
Mom: "Why do you say that?"
Tom: "Because that's what everyone calls me."

> AA-24

THE TALL THIN MAN

Overnight, people all over were talking about Abebe Bikila. That was a name they didn't know just 24 hours before.

It was in 1960. The place was Rome, Italy, and the 1960 Olympic Games were taking place. Many sports lovers were watching the games in Rome and many others were watching on TV.

The Olympic Marathon had just started. In the Marathon, the runners would run a long, long way. They would run for over two hours! Only the very best runner would win. The people watching wondered which runner would come in first.

One of the runners was a tall thin man. Most of the people didn't know his name or where he had come from. But in a little more than two hours, everyone would know his name.

The tall thin man had been a good runner from the time he was a child. His family and friends thought he was one of the best. But now he was running with the best runners from many lands. These runners had planned and worked to run in the Marathon for a long time. Every man wanted to be first. But they didn't know about the tall thin man!

He had started running in shoes like the rest of the runners. But the shoes hurt his feet. He thought he could run faster without shoes, so he stopped and got rid of them.

In only a little time, he ran past one runner. Then he ran past other runners who were starting to tire. And then he saw other runners fall down and stay there. But thanks to all his running as a child, the tall thin man ran now with easy steps.

He ran on and on. Maybe he was thinking of all the times he had run in his mother land. Maybe he was wondering about some of the other runners. Maybe he thought of winning for his homeland. Maybe, without knowing why, he just ran on and on, as fast as he could, down the streets of Rome.

As the men ran, the people watched and waited, talking and wondering who would be the winner. As they waited, night came into the city of Rome.

At last, someone saw the first runner coming. He ran on and on, under the street lights. Everyone looked. They saw that it was the tall thin man! The people started clapping their hands. Some boys ran alongside of the tall thin man. He was the winner of the Olympic Marathon!

"Who is it? Who is the winner? Where is he from?" everyone called.

But no one could tell. Then someone called out, "It's Abebe Bikila! Abebe Bikila is the winner!"

The tall thin man, Abebe Bikila of Ethiopia, was the winner of the 1960 Olympic Marathon. In no time, everyone was talking about Abebe Bikila, one of the best runners ever to run in the Olympic Games.

But Abebe Bikila did not stop running after winning in 1960. Again, in the 1964 Olympics, he was the winner of the Marathon. He was the first ever to win the Olympic Marathon two times!

But the rest of Abebe Bikila's story is very sad. In 1969, he was in a car crash. He was very badly hurt and he could never walk again.

In 1972, the Olympic Marathon was run again. This time, Abebe Bikila could only watch from the side.

Then, in 1973, news came that Abebe Bikila was dead. But people will never forget the tall thin man, for he did something no one ever did before him.

Nan: "Do you know that today there is something wrong with the mind of 1 of every 4 people?"
Ann: "Well, take a good look at 3 of your best friends. If they're OK, then it must be you!"

A driving teacher was teaching a new driver who wasn't doing too well. "There's a little time left," said the teacher. "Let me show you how to fill out accident papers."

AA-25

**It is hard to get older
and have time on your hands.
Here is a letter about one man who finds a
lot of ways to use his time.**

A Letter from Maria

2452 First Street
Middle City, Texas 78240
June 16, 1976

Dear May,

Thank you so much for your letter. It was very kind of you to write. It helps to hear from friends at a time like this.

It is still hard for me to think that Mother is dead. And who would have thought that she would go first. She was only 68. Think of it, Father is 73.

He didn't want to stay in their house, not without Mother. So, he came here to live with us. We thought it would be the best thing for him. But we didn't know that it would be the best thing that ever happened to us.

Now the children are getting to know him well. They love to hear his stories about when he was a boy. When he tells about bringing in wood every day for the cooking fire, they just don't know what to say. And living without being able to turn on hot water . . . that gives them something to think about! They like to be with Father, and it takes his mind off Mother.

As you know, Jim and I work and the children are at school most of the day. We thought it would be hard for Father to have so much time on his hands. At first it was. But Father never could stand around long with nothing to do. Do you remember how much he liked working and fixing things around the house? He is a strong man, and has a lot to do around this house! The other morning I happened to say that the window wouldn't open. By the time I got home that night, the window was fixed. Thanks to Father!

Helping around the house isn't enough for Father. He likes to get out and do things. He has some friends and they like to go to plays, watch baseball, or just go for a walk in the park. The other day they were thinking of getting away for two weeks. We told Father that he should buy some new clothes to take with him. Today he is out shopping for a new shirt.

Now don't you think all this would be enough for one man? But not for Father. He happened to hear that a hospital nearby needed people to help out without getting paid. So now Father is spending two days a week working at the hospital.

We all love and care about Father very much. I hope that he will be with us for a long time.

Thank you again for writing, May. And I hope that you'll come see us in the fall.

Love to all,

Maria

Mr. B: "My son is a writer."
Mr. C: "That's good. Is he writing for money?"
Mr. B: "Oh, yes. Every time he writes a letter to us."

Make Up a Job

What can you do if you don't like working for others? Here are some people who like to do things their way.

Some people don't want to work for others. They want to do things their way. They don't want others telling them what to do, when to do it, and how to do it.

How do these people make a living? They make up jobs to do. How? By looking around and finding things that need doing.

Linda X thought of a way to use cooking and housekeeping to make money.

She went to a nearby hospital and asked for the names of people who need help when they get out of the hospital. Many of them are happy to pay Linda to take care of them.

When they are ready to go home from the hospital, Linda goes with them. She buys the food, cooks it, and talks with them as they eat. She does other things for them, too. She changes the beds, goes to the drugstore, shops, and takes care of the house. Linda has helped many people this way. It's a good job for her.

George Y is young, strong, and not afraid of work. From the time he was a child, George didn't want to work for anyone but George!

George does good work with his hands. So, he goes from house to house, asking what jobs need to be done. He will fix a chair or a table. Or, he will fix things all over the house.

If someone wants a new closet, George can make it. If pipes or steps need fixing, he fixes them. George can do just about anything. He fixes bikes, bells, windows, or anything! You name it, and he'll fix it.

Harry and Anna B knew there must be a way they could make a living on their own. One night when they were sitting and talking, it came to them.

They looked in car lots and got a little truck with one side fixed so it would open up. Then they went out to buy some food. They got buns, nuts, hot and cold meats, and other things to eat, and they put all

this food in the truck. Every weekday they take it to a street where many people work. When the workers want something to eat, they come out and buy from Harry and Anna.

This year, Harry and Anna bet they will take in two times as much money as they would working at jobs.

Betty Z needs money to keep going to school. She's always had pets and knows how to take care of most kinds.

Betty put this ad in the paper: "NEED A PET-SITTER? I care for all kinds, days or overnight. Call 555-9854 and make your pet happy.''

Now Betty walks pets for people who work all day. Sometimes you'll see her in the park walking five at a time!

Betty fixes their food, puts out water for them, and plays with them before she goes home. Sometimes, if people go away, she stays overnight. Betty likes her work because she loves pets.

These are just some of the jobs people can make up. If you're like them, you may want to think about making up a job to fit the way you want to live.

Teacher: ''What can you tell me about the people who lived in the 1700s?''
Ray: ''They are all dead.''

ONE MORE TRY

Steve had the money for Lana, but he gave it to the dirty man. So why did Lana act so nice to Steve?

Steve never thought he would be waiting for Lana, just as he never thought she would call. He had asked her out many times, and she had said "no" every time. "I thought you could help me," she had told Steve when she called. "Could you let me have 20 dollars? I need it in a hurry."

Steve knew what his friends would have said, but he didn't care. He liked Lana and was happy she thought of asking him for help. He would meet her in the park and give her the money.

Then he would ask her out again. "I don't see why we can't meet on the corner," Lana had said, "but if the park does something for you, I'll be there."

Thinking of her words, Steve looked at his watch. He wondered if Lana would show. Just then, a man sat down by Steve. His clothes were dirty, and his hands seemed to be covered with dirt. "Did you ever sleep on the ground in the rain?" he asked.

"No," Steve said, but his thoughts were on Lana.

"I didn't get like this from one rainy day," the man went on, "but now it is spring, and I'm ready to start over. Drink caused my trouble, but I'm done with it. All I drink now comes out of water pipes. I haven't had one other drink in weeks, and I plan to keep away from it."

"You should," Steve said, thinking the man needed help. "Drink and drugs aren't easy to stop."

Then the man told Steve that he wanted to see his family again. "I called," he said, "and they told me to come home. They know I have been sleeping in the park. I said I would come home. First I have to rent a place for a day, run some hot water, and get me and these clothes cleaned up. I want to look and dress a little better than this when I go home."

Steve checked his watch again. Lana wasn't going to show up. "Go rent that place," he said, handing the man 20 dollars.

The man thanked Steve and took the money.

Steve sat there for a time after the man left. He didn't know what had come over him. He had worked too hard for that money to give it away. He just hoped the man got better. Then Lana walked up.

"Let me talk first," she said. "I didn't care to meet here because I was going to come to the park after I had the money. I was going to give the money to a man who has been living here."

Steve started to say something, but Lana put up her hand. "If I had been on time, you would have let me have the money. As it stands, you gave it to the man. I ran into him, and after he told me how he got the money, I knew you gave it to him. The next time you see him, he will look better."

"I don't think I'll see him again," Steve said.

"If you are going to be seeing me," Lana said, "you will see him. He is my father. He dropped out for a long time, but thanks to you, he will be home in a day."

Steve put his arm around Lana. "I knew there was something about the man that I liked," he said.

OUR SUN

You couldn't live without it. What is it? The sun.

Some people say that the sun is mother and father to Earth and all its living things. This is because Earth would be a cold, dead place without the sun. Without the sun, nothing on Earth could live.

All living things need the sun. Without the sun, there would be no food for us to eat. Land and water, day and night . . . all these began because of the sun, and all are needed for anything to live.

The sun makes our time because it makes our day and our night. This is because the Earth is moving all the time, going around and around like a ball. It takes 24 hours for Earth to go around one time. When one side of Earth is to the sun, it is day for that side and night for the other side. Then, as the Earth goes around, the side of the Earth that was in the sunlight moves out of the sunlight. Then it is night on that side of the Earth.

If you look up at the sun, it may not look that big to you. That is because the sun is so far away. But the sun *is* big, much bigger than Earth. From one side of the sun to the other side is about 864,000 miles. From one side of Earth to the other side is about 7,900 miles. It is easy to see that the sun is many, many times bigger than Earth.

The sun is not like Earth. There is no land or water on the sun. There is no day or night. The sun is nothing but a big ball of fire. Some of the hot light from the sun comes across the 93,000,000 miles to us on Earth.

This hot light from the sun makes Earth the way it is. If something should happen to the sun and Earth did not get its light, Earth would get cold fast. Then all living things on Earth would be dead in a little time.

Or, if the sun should change and get much hotter, Earth, too, would get hotter. If Earth got much hotter, living things could not live. This way, too, Earth and everything on it would be dead.

Did you know that the sun has storms? It does—fire storms! They are bigger than any storm you'll ever see on Earth, and much hotter too. No storm on Earth has ever been as strong as a sun storm.

If you stay out in the hot sun too long, it can make you sick. You think that you're on fire! And you must never look right at the sun. Why not? Your eyes may go bad, and you may never see again.

But on the other hand, think of all the good things the sun does for us. Sometimes it can make sick people well. Many sick people go off to sunny countries to live and to rest. These people may start to get better right away.

The sun is so important in our lives that we have named the first day of the week for it—Sunday.

John got on the bus and said to Ron, "I want to get off the bus at Park Street. How will I know when to get off?"

"Easy," said Ron. "Just watch me, and get off the bus two stops before I do."

THE AMERICAN COWBOY

What was it like in the days of the American cowboy? Not the way we see it on TV!

After looking at TV shows, most of us think the American cowboy was something like this: He was tall, good-looking, and his face was always tanned. His clothes were always neat and clean and his hat always looked new. He pulled out his gun at the drop of a hat. And he was so good with it that he could drill a dime from across the room. He got in fights all the time and beat any man he had a fight with. He always got the girl and they always rode off into the sunset, singing and looking happy about everything.

But was the American cowboy like this? "No, far from it," say the people who have checked into the days when the American cowboy herded livestock for weeks at a time over miles and miles of country.

The big years of the American cowboy were from about 1867 to 1887. In this time, about 40,000 of them rode for a living out in the West. Most cowboys were only 18 or 19, little more than boys. But some were in their 20s and 30s. Some had come from farms, some had been fighters in the Civil War, some had worked on boats, and some had come to the U.S. from other countries. One-third of them were American Indians, Blacks, or Mexicans.

The American cowboy's job was hard, tiring, and filled with danger. He rode mile after mile, day after day, with his herd. He worked in the heat of the sun, in driving rain, and in cold from which he could not escape.

He was always dusty and dirty. That was because there wasn't much water out where he had to spend his time.

He worked long hours. Most of the time he put in an 18-hour day, 7 days a week. And for this he got only $25.00 a month—with room and board. The room wasn't much and the food was bad. Often he joked and laughed about these things with his friends.

He worked outdoors all year round. Cold or hot, he was out working. And if he got sick or hurt, he had something to worry about because he had no one to turn to for help. There were no doctors around.

Sometimes a cowboy would come upon a friend where he lay dead from sickness, somewhere out in the open country.

Most of the American cowboys were not gunmen and most had never shot anyone. One long-time cowboy said he never saw anyone draw a gun on a man in all the time he rode herd. The cowboy's job was to herd livestock and that's what he did!

As for women? Well, most of the time there weren't any where the cowboy worked. When he drove the herd to a city, the cowboy could meet some women. Maybe, just like on TV, one or two cowboys rode off into the sunset with a girl, but not many!

But whatever the American cowboys were like, we do know this: From 1867 to 1887 they drove over 5,000,000 cattle to the cities. And they rode their way into the American story for all time.

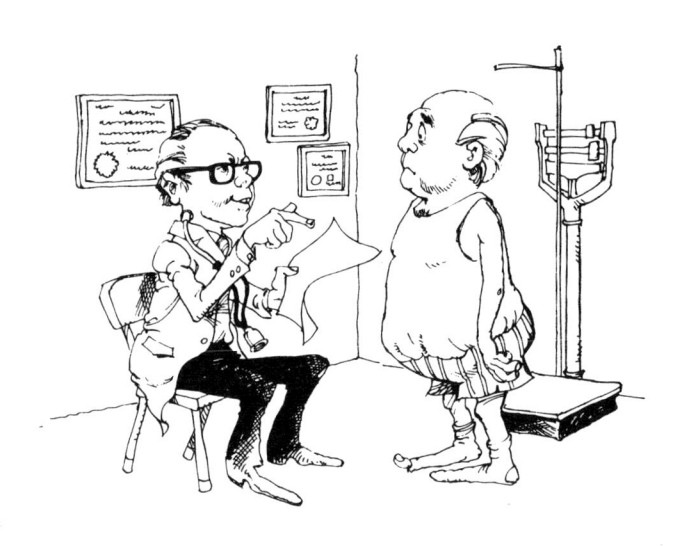

"I will let you eat everything you like. And here are the things that you are going to like. . . ."

YOUNG DRINKERS

Drinking sometimes looks like the thing to do.

But

there are dangers in drinking.

From the first times we know about, people have always done some drinking. And drinking has always troubled many people. People everywhere are drinking more and more these days. But the thing that is most upsetting is that now there are many young drinkers, drinkers who are under 20 years old.

On the way to school, some young people are sitting in the back of the bus. They're drinking, and it's not 7-UP! In the park, boys, 9 and 12, are watching a ball game. They are drinking from cans that are covered up with T-shirts. Down the street, five girls are at home watching TV. They are drinking too.

One newspaper says that in the U.S., over 1,000,000 boys and girls from 12 to 17 drink so much that they are in danger from their drinking. Some cannot stop drinking and it could be that some will be dead from it before they are out of school.

The police say they now catch 3 times as many young people for drinking and driving as they did in 1967. And more and more car accidents happen with young drivers who have been drinking.

One-third of the young people who drink say they drive cars when they have had more than five drinks. So, it's easy to see why so many young people are dead because of drinking/driving accidents. In nearly two-thirds of these accidents, the dead people are under 20 years old.

Not so many young people use hard drugs anymore. Drink does not cost as much as drugs, and it is very easy to get. What most people don't know is that drink is a drug. And it is as easy to get "hooked" on drink as it is on other drugs.

Doctors are trying to find out why young people are drinking more. They are finding that some drink just because it is the "in" thing to do. Others drink because they are afraid not to. They are afraid their friends will laugh at them and call them children because they do not drink. Others drink because they think it makes them look older. And others drink because they say a drink makes it easy for them to laugh and tell jokes. They say it makes them feel good. "It makes my head feel light," says one boy.

Drinking is hurting so many young people's health that now there are classes to teach them how not to drink. In these classes, people learn that they don't have to be afraid of what others think of them. They learn how to talk and joke with others . . . without drinking. And they learn what can happen when they drink and drive. Many classes show car accidents that have happened. Sometimes looking at these car accidents makes the people in the classes so sick that they pass out.

Today many young people are learning how to get along without drinking. What about you? Do you drink? If you do, think about it! What does it do for you? What can it do to you and to your friends?

Inside Me

Can people look inside and see
That I have feelings inside of me?
Do they know I have good days and bad
Some days I'm happy, some days sad?
Do they know it's hard to make my way
To keep on trying every day?
Do they understand? How can they know
What makes me run? What makes me go?

A man walked into a doctor's place with a duck on his head.

"You need help," the doctor said.

"You bet I do," the duck said. "Get this man out from under me!"

AA-1 — THE CLEANER

Read each sentence. Write <u>Yes</u>, <u>No</u>, or <u>?</u> for every one.
1. _____ Sometimes women clean the buses.
2. _____ Ken likes to show that he knows everything.
3. _____ One of Bob's jobs is to clean the buses.
4. _____ Bob knows Ken.
5. _____ Ken got the cleaner at the store.
6. _____ Ken's cleaner is good.
7. _____ Janet helps Ken clean the bus.
8. _____ Ken did a good job.
9. _____ The cleaner got the bus wet.

Find the one correct answer.

10. _____ What is the story about?
    a. Ken has a job cleaning buses.
    b. All work and no pay for Ken
    c. Getting a good cleaner at the store

Check on page 132

AA-2 — FIRED FOR SMOKING

Read each sentence. Write <u>Yes</u>, <u>No</u>, or <u>?</u> for every one.
1. _____ Bill looked happy.
2. _____ Bill was a good worker.
3. _____ Bill and Kay are good friends.
4. _____ Fires start fast at jobs like Bill's.

Show what goes with every one.

5. ____ Bill may not smoke
6. ____ A fire can put workers
7. ____ The workers may smoke
8. ____ Bill asks Kay
9. ____ Bill didn't know they fire workers

a. out the exits.
b. for one last smoke.
c. at his job.
d. for smoking.
e. in the hospital.

Find the one correct answer.

10. ____ What is the story about?
   a. Bill smokes at the exits.
   b. Bill is fired for smoking.
   c. Bill stops smoking.

Check on page 132

AA-3 ━━━━━━━━━ WHAT A MORNING!

Read each sentence. Write <u>Yes</u>, <u>No</u>, or <u>?</u> for every one.

1. ____ Rosita's job is cashing checks.
2. ____ The 2 men wanted to help Rosita with her work.
3. ____ Rosita got the men to go into the safe with her.
4. ____ The men got what they wanted and got out of the safe fast!
5. ____ The men and women outside the safe could see what was happening on a TV.

When did the things happen in the story? Show it by writing 1, 2, 3, and 4.

6. ___ A TV shows what is going on inside the safe.
7. ___ The men asked Rosita for cash.
8. ___ Rosita goes into the safe with the men.
9. ___ They get the men and Rosita is OK.

Find the one correct answer.

10. ___ What is the story about?
    a. The morning is over and Rosita didn't do her work.
    b. Rosita thought it out and helped get the men.
    c. It was good to have cash in a safe.

Check on page 132

AA-4 — HELP FOR TWO

Read each sentence. Write Yes, No, or ? for every one.
1. ___ Linda Chan worked at the hospital.
2. ___ Linda did cleaning at the hospital.
3. ___ George Wah wanted to tell Linda a story.
4. ___ Linda did not have time for George's story.
5. ___ Linda liked George's doctor.
6. ___ George played baseball in the hospital.

Show what goes with every one.

7. ___ Linda and the doctor
8. ___ Linda
9. ___ Linda and George
10. ___ George

a. talked about help.
b. asked for help.
c. helped George.
d. talked about George.

When did the things happen in the story? Show it by writing 1, 2, 3, and 4.

11. ___ Linda liked her job.
12. ___ George was put in the hospital.
13. ___ Linda went to see George's doctor.
14. ___ George told a story.

Find the correct answer.

15. ___ A good new name for this story could be
    a. "Linda at Work."
    b. "A Walk with George."
    c. "Linda Learns about Work."

Check on page 132

AA-5 — JACK HITS IT HOME

Read each sentence. Write <u>Yes</u>, <u>No</u>, or <u>?</u> for every one.
1. ____ Jack could see the ball lot from his window.
2. ____ Jack was a good player, so the men wanted him to play with them.
3. ____ The men played ball every night.
4. ____ Jack hit a home run.
5. ____ The bat hit Jack's window.

Show what goes with every one.

6. ____ Jack paid a lot
7. ____ The window looked good
8. ____ Jack went to bat
9. ____ The ball went

a. from the outside.
b. into Jack's window.
c. for his window.
d. for his side.

Find the one correct answer.

10. ____ What is the story about?
    a. A hit Jack didn't want
    b. Jack hit a home run.
    c. Jack played ball at night.

Check on page 132

AA-6 CHECK THAT STORY

Read each sentence. Write <u>Yes</u>, <u>No</u>, or <u>?</u> for every one.
1. _____ Angela thought Tony was in trouble.
2. _____ Ed did see Tony break into the drugstore.
3. _____ Jim takes the bus to work.
4. _____ Tony was running from the police.
5. _____ Ed put things together without thinking.
6. _____ Jim says he isn't going to tell a story again without checking.

When did this happen in the story? Show it by writing 1, 2, 3, and 4.
7. _____ Jim thinks Tony is on drugs.
8. _____ Angela sees Tony running in the street.
9. _____ The doctor tells Jim that Tony was running for the bus.
10. _____ Jim asks Ed about Tony.

Write one of the names from the box in every blank.

| Dr. Clayton |
| Jim |
| Tony |
| Angela |

11. Jim stops to talk with _____ on her way to work.
12. _____ was running in the street to get the bus.
13. _____ looked like he was going to have a fit!
14. The story about Tony was put together by _____.

Find the one correct answer.

15. _____ What is the story about?
    a. Men and women who ride the bus to work
    b. Jim's seeing Ed on his way to work
    c. What can happen when a story isn't checked out

Check on page 132

AA-7 ━━━━━━━━━━━━━━━ HELP! FIRE!

Read each sentence. Write <u>Yes</u>, <u>No</u>, or <u>?</u> for every one.
1. _____ The Goodsons now live over the drugstore.
2. _____ The Goodsons didn't like the home they had.
3. _____ Mr. Goodson wasn't looking where he was going, and that's why the bus hit him.
4. _____ Mr. Goodson will walk again.
5. _____ Ed went into the fire to help get Mr. Goodson out.
6. _____ Ed, Mary, Dan, and Mr. Goodson sat on the sidewalk so that they could watch the fire.
7. _____ When the fire fighters got to the home, they put out the fire.
8. _____ Mr. Goodson said he got out of the fire without help.
9. _____ Dan and Ed are good friends.
10. _____ Ed wasn't thinking about being safe when he went to help Mr. Goodson.

When did this happen in the story? Show it by writing 1, 2, 3, and 4.

11. _____ The TV people asked Ed, "Why did you go into all that smoke and fire?"
12. _____ Ed could see smoke inside the window.
13. _____ Many people watched the fire.
14. _____ Mary was telling Ed not to let the fire get him.

Find the one correct answer.

(15.) _____ What is the story about?
  a. Mr. Goodson gets hit by a bus after getting a good job.
  b. A fire starts at the drugstore.
  c. The Kennans help out when a fire starts.

Check on page 133

AA-8 ══════════════ *THAT MR. BRUNO!*

Read each sentence. Write Yes, No, or ? for every one.

1. _____ There are not many things to buy in Mr. Bruno's store.
2. _____ Mr. Bruno has help in his store.
3. _____ Mr. Bruno finds books for people.
4. _____ Mr. Bruno likes to fight with all the people in his store.
5. _____ Mr. Bruno went to a school for people who can't see.
6. _____ Children will not go into Mr. Bruno's store.
7. _____ Julio and Maria went to a show last night.
8. _____ Julio and Maria had a fight.
9. _____ Mr. Bruno knows a lot about everything.

Show what goes with every one.

10. ___ Mr. Bruno can't
11. ___ Mr. Bruno knows
12. ___ Mr. Bruno can help
13. ___ Julio was not
14. ___ Jill Farmer and Mike Day work

a. where all the things are.
b. people find books.
c. see.
d. for Mr. Bruno.
e. happy.

Find the one correct answer.

15. ___ What is the story about?
   a. A good way to run a store
   b. Finding things in a store with no help
   c. A man who can't see, but can do many things

Check on page 133

AA-9 — TROUBLE RIDE

Read each sentence. Write <u>Yes</u>, <u>No</u>, or <u>?</u> for every one.

1. ___ The boy didn't like school.
2. ___ The bus was going to LA.
3. ___ The boy was with his parents.
4. ___ The policeman liked his work.
5. ___ The bus stopped in Barstow.

When did things happen in the story? Show it by writing 1, 2, 3, and 4.
6. ___ The boy asked for help.
7. ___ The bus got to LA.
8. ___ A man got on the bus.
9. ___ The boy talked about his parents.

Find the one correct answer.

10. ___ A good new name for this story could be
    a. "Ride to LA."
    b. "Stop the Bus."
    c. "The Story the Boy Didn't Tell."

Check on page 133

AA-10 ━━━ PETE GETS IT TOGETHER

Read each sentence. Write Yes, No, or ? for every one.
1. ___ Pete fell over things a lot.
2. ___ Many boys liked to play with Pete.
3. ___ Pete did good work at school.
4. ___ Pete had a fight on the way home from school.
5. ___ Pete and Sue went to school together.
6. ___ Sue liked it that Pete didn't talk a lot.

Read each sentence. Show who said it by writing the correct letter.

7. _____ "I watched you put that garbage in the can."
8. _____ "I like clean streets."
9. _____ "Get lost. We don't want you."

a. The boys
b. Sue
c. Pete

Find the one correct answer.

10. _____ A good new name for this story could be
    a. "Pete Finds a Friend."
    b. "The Garbage Man."
    c. "Clean Streets."

Check on page 133

AA-11 ━━━━━━━━━━━ EVE GETS GOING

Read each sentence. Write <u>Yes</u>, <u>No</u>, or <u>?</u> for every one.

1. _____ Eve lost her job.
2. _____ Eve was over 30.
3. _____ Eve worked in a hospital.
4. _____ Eve lived in a boarding house.
5. _____ Eve had a fight with her landlord.
6. _____ Eve gave Mrs. Cook her last rent.

Read each sentence. Show what goes with every one.

7. _____ When Eve lost her job she was
8. _____ On her way home Eve was sad and
9. _____ When Eve told Mrs. Cook she was going, Eve was

a. happy.
b. mad.
c. tired.

Find the one correct answer.

10. _____ A good name for this story could be
   a. "Eve Can Do It!"
   b. "A Sad Day for Eve."
   c. "Good Friends Help Eve."

Check on page 133

AA-12 ━━━━━WHAT GOOD ARE TAXES?

Read each sentence. Write <u>Yes</u>, <u>No</u>, or <u>?</u> for every one.

1. _____ Taxes are money everyone has to pay, one way or the other.
2. _____ We pay taxes on many things we buy in stores.
3. _____ If you forget to pay your taxes, you are in bad trouble.
4. _____ If you don't have a house, you get out of paying taxes.
5. _____ The city pays the police with tax money.

Read each sentence. Read the words in the box. Find the word that goes in every sentence.

> ball   schools   Health   clean

6. Tax money pays for new _____.
7. Taxes help pay the people who keep the streets _____.
8. Taxes pay the people working at the Board of _____.
9. Taxes help pay for the lot you play _____ in.

Find the one correct answer.

10. _____ A good new name for this story could be
    a. "Pat Hears a Story."
    b. "No More Taxes."
    c. "Ramon Learns about Taxes."

Check on page 133

AA-13 — CAN LOVE LAST?

Read each sentence. Write Yes, No, or ? for every one.

1. _____ James said school was all Alice thought about.
2. _____ James's parents want him to stay in school.
3. _____ Alice wants to stop going to school.
4. _____ Sally and Joe are working things out.
5. _____ James will keep going to school so Alice will be happy.

Find the one that tells the meaning of what was said.

6. ____ "School isn't where it's at."
   a. James didn't like school.
   b. James had a job.
   c. School is for children.

8. ____ "Please, James, think things over."
   a. Alice wants James to get a job.
   b. Alice wants James to keep going to school.
   c. Alice wants James to take her out.

7. ____ "Love went right out the window for them."
   a. Sally and Joe are not together.
   b. Alice does not love James.
   c. Alice and James went away together.

9. ____ "You do that and I'll do what's right for me."
   a. Alice will talk to Sally.
   b. Alice will go to work.
   c. Alice and James might not stay together.

Find the one correct answer.

10. ____ A good new name for this story could be
    a. "Walking to School."
    b. "Thinking Things Over."
    c. "Being Like Sally and Joe."

Check on page 134

110

AA-14 ——————— TWO WEEKS TOGETHER

Read each sentence. Write <u>Yes</u>, <u>No</u>, or <u>?</u> for every one.

1. _____ June and Ed are good friends with Pedro and Maria.
2. _____ June and Maria work together.
3. _____ Ed and Pedro work in a school.
4. _____ Ed and Pedro will be home from work for 5 weeks.
5. _____ They all talk it over. They will be at home one week and will go somewhere the other week.

Show what goes with every one.

6. _____ Ed said,
7. _____ June said,
8. _____ Maria said,
9. _____ Pedro said,

a. "Where do you want to go, Ed?"
b. "Pedro and I will not be working for two weeks."
c. "If we are going somewhere, we have to plan."
d. "Come on in and let me have your coats."

111

Find the one correct answer.

10. ____ What is this story about?
    a. The women want to go away, and the men want to stay home.
    b. You can have fun at home when you are with friends.
    c. Good friends think of a good plan for the time they have off from work.

Check on page 134

AA-15 ━━━━━━DON'T BUY TROUBLE

Show what goes with every one.

1. ____ Will Walker
2. ____ The newspaper
3. ____ Bellson's Store
4. ____ The "bargain" salesman
5. ____ The police

a. has coats to sell.
b. wanted to buy a coat.
c. was asked to help.
d. want to find the man.
e. has to be stopped.

When did things happen in the story? Show it by writing 1, 2, 3, and 4.

6. ____ Walker goes to the police station.
7. ____ Walker waits for the "bargain" salesman and the coat.
8. ____ Walker looks at coats in Bellson's window.
9. ____ Walker gives money to the "bargain" salesman.

Find the one correct answer.

10. _____ A good new name for the story could be
   a. "Walker and the Bargain Salesman."
   b. "The Police Ask for Help."
   c. "Walker Buys a New Coat."

Check on page 134

AA-16 — TWO LOVES

Read each sentence. Write <u>Yes</u>, <u>No</u>, or <u>?</u> for every one.

1. _____ Tim wants to keep his car looking good.
2. _____ Sue knows how to drive.
3. _____ This is Tim's first car.
4. _____ Tim and Sue are in love.
5. _____ Tim and Sue talked a lot about Sue's learning to drive.
6. _____ Tim wants Sue to go to driving school.

When did things happen in the story? Show it by writing 1, 2, 3, and 4.

7. _____ Sue wants to drive the car.
8. _____ Tim buys a new car.
9. _____ Tim tells Sue to go to driving school.
10. _____ Tim goes to Sue's for supper.

Read each sentence. Read the words in the box. Find the word that goes in every sentence.

> teacher   car   bus   girl

11. Tim takes the _____ to work.
12. Sue wants to drive the new _____.
13. Sue is Tim's _____.
14. Tim wants Sue to learn with a good _____.

Find the one correct answer.

(15.) _____ What is this story about?
   a. Tim gives Sue a ring, and they plan to buy a car for her.
   b. Tim finds a way to keep his car safe and let his girl friend learn to drive.
   c. Sue and Tim have a bad fight because of Tim's car.

Check on page 134

AA-17 ──────────────── THAT'S MY JOB

Read each sentence. Write <u>Yes</u>, <u>No</u>, or <u>?</u> for every one.
1. _____ The mailman likes to walk.
2. _____ There is little mail to give out on Monday.
3. _____ The mailman goes home at 6 every night.
4. _____ You can make a lot of new friends when you're a mailman.
5. _____ The mailman drives a new car.

Show what goes with each one.
6. _____ June Story
7. _____ Mrs. Mano
8. _____ Mr. Sellers
9. _____ The mailman

a. gets many bills.
b. has a son who is in New City.
c. likes his job.
d. gets a letter from her boyfriend.

Find the one correct answer.

(10.) _____ A good new name for this story could be
a. "A Letter from New City."
b. "The Ups and Downs of Being a Mailman."
c. "Too Many Bills for Mr. Sellers."

Check on page 134

AA-18 ══════════════════ IT'S A STEAL

Read each sentence. Write Yes, No, or ? for each one.
1. _____ People steal at big stores and little stores.
2. _____ Sometimes people steal for fun.
3. _____ All people need the things they steal.
4. _____ Only children steal from stores.
5. _____ Costs go up because people steal from stores.
6. _____ Many people sell what they steal.

115

Find all of the correct answers.

7. Who are the people who steal from stores?
   - _____ a. Children
   - _____ b. Salespeople
   - _____ c. People who have money
   - _____ d. Storekeepers
   - _____ e. People up to 80 and over

Find the correct answer.

8. Who pays for the things people steal?
   - _____ a. The people who do the stealing
   - _____ b. The police
   - _____ c. All of us

9. One newspaper says that
   - _____ a. every other buyer steals.
   - _____ b. one buyer out of 15 steals.
   - _____ c. most stealing is done by salespeople.

10. _____ What is this story about?
    - a. Trouble for the police
    - b. Why stealing costs us all money
    - c. School children learning to steal

Check on page 134

AA-19 — A MAN FINDS A JOB

Read each sentence. Write <u>Yes</u>, <u>No</u>, or <u>?</u> for every one.

1. _____ Rusty is 18.
2. _____ Rusty worked as a salesman.
3. _____ Rusty learned how to work on cars in school.
4. _____ Rusty and Chuck worked on the car.
5. _____ The car Rusty fixed was Chuck's car.

When did things happen in the story? Show it by writing 1, 2, 3, and 4.

6. _____ Rusty happened to hear that Chuck's Corner Station needed help.
7. _____ The man in the store calls Rusty a boy.
8. _____ Chuck gives Rusty a job.
9. _____ Rusty and Chuck go for a drive in the car to see what needs to be fixed.

Find the one correct answer.

10. _____ What is this story about?
    a. A boy gets a job fixing cars at Chuck's Corner Station.
    b. A man calls Rusty a boy when he finds out that Rusty is only 18.
    c. Rusty, who is 18, shows that he is a man, not a boy.

Check on page 135

AA-20 —————————————— THE GOLD DOOR

Read each sentence. Write Yes, No, or ? for every one.

1. _____ An old man was handing out little papers.
2. _____ All the papers said "Eat At Joe's."
3. _____ The old man was not in good health.
4. _____ The storyteller ran into a store.
5. _____ The girl was about to jump out the window.
6. _____ The girl had lots of money.
7. _____ All the doors in the house were gold.
8. _____ The old man had left before the storyteller could talk to him.
9. _____ "The Gold Door" is the name of a play.

Show what goes with each one.

10. _____ The old man
11. _____ The big sign
12. _____ The storyteller
13. _____ The girl in the house
14. _____ A friend of the old man

a. said "I can help you."
b. had sad eyes.
c. was going to be in a play.
d. said "I work for Joe."
e. said "Opening Monday—The Gold Door."

Find the one correct answer.

15. _____ A good new name for this story could be
    a. "Working for Joe."
    b. "Why Is She Going to Jump?"
    c. "Who Knows Why Things Happen?"

Check on page 135

AA-21 ━━━━━━━━━━━━━━━━━━ RIGHT ON!

Read each sentence. Write Yes, No, or ? for every one.

1. _____ June and Ann like their food store.
2. _____ June and Ann went to the same school.
3. _____ Their plan was to let dollars talk to the storekeeper.
4. _____ A store needs many shoppers to make money.

When did things happen in the story? Show it by writing 1, 2, 3, 4, and 5.

5. _____ The newspaper sent someone over for a story.
6. _____ June and Ann get mad and work out a plan.
7. _____ The storekeeper said he would get better things and keep the store clean.
8. _____ They told 20 friends about their plan.
9. _____ The women got together to make signs.

Find the correct answer.

10. _____ What is this story about?
    a. When many people work together, they can right a wrong.
    b. Women like to go shopping.
    c. The storekeeper makes more money.

Check on page 135

AA-22 — EVERYTHING HAPPENS TO MIKE

Read each sentence. Write Yes, No, or ? for every one.

1. _____ Mike has had five falls in the last two weeks.
2. _____ There was a "Danger" sign at the cleaners.
3. _____ Gus told Mike to see an eye doctor.
4. _____ The eye doctor didn't help Mike.
5. _____ Mike wanted to go back to look at the sign.
6. _____ The eye doctor wanted to see Mike one more time.

Read each sentence. Read the words in the box. Find the word that goes in each sentence.

> cleaners   hospital   sign

7. Mike was at the _____ so many times, everyone there knew him.
8. Mike couldn't see the _____.
9. Mike fell down at the _____.

Find the one correct answer.

10. _____ What is this story about?
   a. Mike has many accidents because he can't see well.
   b. Mike likes going to the hospital.
   c. Gus can't help his friend Mike.

Check on page 135

AA-23 — THE CRASH

Read each sentence. Write <u>Yes</u>, <u>No</u>, or <u>?</u> for every one.

1. _____ A car just missed hitting Jan Coats.
2. _____ Jan was walking home from her job at the food store.
3. _____ Jan and the man got the people out of the cars.
4. _____ The policeman said the drivers must have been going too fast to stop.
5. _____ One of the drivers will not live.

After the crash, when did things happen in the story? Show it by writing 1, 2, 3, 4, and 5.

6. ____ Jan told the man to call the police.
7. ____ The police car pulled up.
8. ____ Jan ran to a nearby house and started ringing the bell.
9. ____ The doctors got the people out of the cars.
10. ____ Together Jan and the man got both doors open.

Read each sentence. Show who said it by writing the correct letter.

11. ____ "Help! Help! I need help!"
12. ____ "Let's try to get the doors open."
13. ____ "It's good that you didn't move them."
14. ____ "Driving too fast doesn't pay."

a. The policeman
b. The doctor
c. The man who was sleeping
d. Jan

Find the one correct answer.

15. ____ What is this story about?
    a. Men drive too fast.
    b. It's easy to drive at night.
    c. Fast work can save lives in an accident.

Check on page 135

AA-24 — THE TALL THIN MAN

Read each sentence. Write <u>Yes</u>, <u>No</u>, or <u>?</u> for every one.

1. _____ In the Marathon, runners run for over two hours.
2. _____ The tall thin man could not run well when he was a child.
3. _____ Abebe Bikila had never come in first before winning the Marathon.
4. _____ Abebe Bikila was the first ever to win the Olympic Marathon two times.
5. _____ Right after the car crash in 1969, news came that Abebe Bikila was dead.

Show what goes with every one.

6. _____ In 1964
7. _____ In 1969
8. _____ In 1960
9. _____ In 1972

a. Abebe Bikila won the Marathon for the first time.
b. Abebe Bikila was the first ever to win the Marathon two times.
c. Abebe Bikila could only watch the Marathon from the side.
d. Abebe Bikila was in a car crash.

Find the one correct answer.

10. ____ A good new name for this story could be
   a. "A Winner."
   b. "The Olympic Marathon."
   c. "The Streets of Rome."

Check on page 135

AA-25 ━━━━━ A LETTER FROM MARIA

Read each sentence. Write <u>Yes</u>, <u>No</u>, or <u>?</u> for every one.

1. ____ The children love to hear Father's stories.
2. ____ Jim and Maria work together.
3. ____ Father used to be a storekeeper.
4. ____ Father can't find things to do with his time.
5. ____ Father gets good pay working at the hospital.

Read each sentence. Read the words in the box. Find the word that goes in every sentence.

> shirt   hospital   window   children

6. The _____ are getting to know Father well.
7. Father fixed the _____ .
8. Father went shopping for a new _____ .
9. Father helps out at the _____ .

Find the one correct answer.

10. _____ A good new name for this story could be
   a. "Jim and Maria."
   b. "Getting to Know Him."
   c. "Living with Father."

Check on page 136

AA-26 ═══════════ MAKE UP A JOB

Show what goes with every one.

1. _____ George Y
2. _____ Betty Z
3. _____ Harry and Anna B
4. _____ Linda X

   a. helps people coming home from the hospital.
   b. fixes things in people's homes.
   c. takes care of pets for people.
   d. sell food to workers.

Find the correct answer.

5. _____ George is the kind of person who
   a. can do anything with his hands.
   b. likes to take care of pets.
   c. gets along well with everyone.

6. _____ Linda most likely
   a. likes to watch TV.
   b. wants money for new clothes.
   c. is kind and gets along with people.

7. ___ Harry and Anna
   a. know how to fix up a truck.
   b. know what workers like to eat.
   c. like to fix things around the house.

8. ___ From her job you can tell that Betty
   a. loves most kinds of pets.
   b. must be afraid of cats.
   c. likes working with people.

9. ___ All the people in the story
   a. live near one another.
   b. went to the same school.
   c. made up jobs that were right for them.

(10.) ___ A good new name for this story could be
   a. "Linda Finds a Way."
   b. "Do It Your Way!"
   c. "George Can Fix It."

Check on page 136

AA-27 ONE MORE TRY

Read each sentence. Write Yes, No, or ? for every one.
1. ___ Steve wanted to meet Lana.
2. ___ Lana thought of meeting Steve in the park.
3. ___ The man who sat by Steve was clean.
4. ___ Steve was falling in love with Lana.

125

Find all the correct answers.

5. What things made Steve think about giving the money away?
   ___ a. The story the man told him.
   ___ b. The man looked like Lana.
   ___ c. Steve didn't think he would see Lana.
   ___ d. It was a rainy day.
   ___ e. Steve didn't want his friends to get the money.

When did the things happen in the story? Show it by writing 1, 2, 3, and 4.

6. ___ A man sat by Steve.
7. ___ Steve went to the park.
8. ___ Lana called Steve.
9. ___ Steve learned who the man was.

Find the correct answer.

10. ___ A good name for the story could be
    a. "All in the Family."
    b. "Lana's Last Call."
    c. "A Good Day for All."

Check on page 136

AA-28 — OUR SUN

Read each sentence. Read the words in the box. Find the word or words that go in every sentence.

> fire   93,000,000 miles   time
> Earth   24 hours   864,000 miles

1. Without the sun, nothing on _____ could live.
2. The sun makes our _____ because it makes our day and our night.
3. It takes _____ for Earth to go around one time.
4. It is _____ from the sun to the Earth.
5. From one side of the sun to the other side is about _____.
6. The sun is nothing but a big ball of _____.

Find all the correct answers.
7. What are sun storms like?
   _____ a. They are bigger than any storm you'll see on Earth.
   _____ b. They bring a lot of rain.
   _____ c. They are very strong.
   _____ d. They are very hot.
   _____ e. They are very cold.

Find the one correct answer.

8. ____ If you stay out in the sun for a long time,
   a. nothing bad will happen to you.
   b. it can make you sick.
   c. you will be in the middle of a sun storm.

9. ____ The sun
   a. is nothing but trouble for the people on Earth.
   b. does more bad things than good things for us.
   c. does more good things than bad things for us.

10. ____ What is this story about?
    a. How the sun can make you sick
    b. Why the sun is important to Earth
    c. Why the sun is not like Earth

Check on page 136

AA-29 ▬▬▬▬▬THE AMERICAN COWBOY

Read each sentence. Write a if the sentence tells a fact about the American cowboy. Write b if the sentence tells how TV shows the American cowboy.

    a. A fact   **b. What TV shows**

1. ____ They had to spend their days herding livestock.
2. ____ They were all tall, tan, and good-looking.
3. ____ They were all fast with a gun.
4. ____ Many cowboys were Black, Mexican, or American Indian.

5. _____ They worked long hours and got little pay.
6. _____ Their clothes and hats were always clean and new.
7. _____ They always got the girl.

Find all the correct answers.

8. Where did the cowboys come from?
   _____ a. Some came from farms.
   _____ b. Some had been fighters in the Civil War.
   _____ c. Some were doctors.
   _____ d. Some had worked on boats.
   _____ e. Some had come from other countries.
   _____ f. Some worked on TV shows.

Find the one correct answer.

9. _____ What kind of man would be a cowboy?
   a. A tall, good-looking man
   b. A man who liked to do things the easy way
   c. A hard-worker who wasn't afraid to face danger

10. _____ What is this story about?
    a. What the American cowboy was like
    b. The American cowboy as we see him on TV
    c. How to herd livestock

Check on page 136

AA-30 ━━━━━━━━━YOUNG DRINKERS

Read each sentence. Write <u>Yes</u>, <u>No</u>, or <u>?</u> for every one.
1. _____ Drivers who drink put others in danger.
2. _____ The health of drinkers is in danger.
3. _____ Drink is not a drug.
4. _____ New classes help young people think about and know more about drinking.
5. _____ People aren't drinking as much these days.
6. _____ More young people were picked up for drinking in 1967 than today.

Show what goes with every one.
7. _____ One-third
8. _____ Nearly two-thirds
9. _____ Over 1,000,000

a. boys and girls from 12 to 17 in the U.S. drink so much that they are in danger.
b. of the young people who drink say they drive cars when they have had more than five drinks.
c. of drinking/driving accidents have dead people under 20 years old.

Read each sentence. Read the words in the box. Find the word that goes in every sentence.

> light   children   older   "in"

10. Doctors find that some young people drink just because it is the _____ thing to do.
11. Others are afraid their friends will call them _____.
12. Others drink because they think it makes them look _____.
13. One boy drinks because it makes his head feel _____.

Find the one correct answer.

14. _____ From reading the story, you can tell that the writer wants young people
    a. to stop drinking.
    b. to stay in school.
    c. to go to school to learn how to drive.

15. _____ What is the story about?
    a. How to stop drinking
    b. Car accidents
    c. Young people and drinking

Check on page 136

Comprehension Questions Answer Key

AA-1
1. ?
2. Yes
3. Yes
4. Yes
5. Yes
6. Yes
7. No
8. Yes
9. ?
10. b

AA-2
1. No
2. Yes
3. ?
4. Yes
5. c
6. e
7. a
8. b
9. d
10. b

AA-3
1. Yes
2. No
3. Yes
4. No
5. Yes
6. 3
7. 1
8. 2
9. 4
10. b

AA-4
1. Yes
2. ?
3. Yes
4. No
5. ?
6. No
7. d
8. c
9. a
10. b
11. 4
12. 1
13. 3
14. 2
15. c

AA-5
1. Yes
2. ?
3. Yes
4. Yes
5. No
6. c
7. a
8. d
9. b
10. a

AA-6
1. Yes
2. No
3. ?
4. No
5. No
6. Yes
7. 3
8. 1
9. 4
10. 2
11. Angela
12. Tony
13. Doctor Clayton
14. Jim
15. c

AA-7

1. Yes
2. No
3. ?
4. No
5. Yes
6. No
7. Yes
8. No
9. ?
10. Yes
11. 4
12. 1
13. 3
14. 2
15. c

AA-8

1. No
2. Yes
3. Yes
4. No
5. ?
6. No
7. ?
8. Yes
9. Yes
10. c
11. a
12. b
13. e
14. d
15. c

AA-9

1. ?
2. Yes
3. No
4. ?
5. Yes
6. 3
7. 4
8. 1
9. 2
10. c

AA-10

1. Yes
2. No
3. ?
4. No
5. Yes
6. Yes
7. b
8. c
9. a
10. a

AA-11

1. Yes
2. ?
3. No
4. Yes
5. No
6. Yes
7. b. mad
8. c. tired
9. a. happy
10. a

AA-12

1. Yes
2. Yes
3. ?
4. No
5. Yes
6. schools
7. clean
8. Health
9. ball
10. c

AA-13

1. Yes
2. ?
3. No
4. No
5. ?
6. a
7. a
8. b
9. c
10. b

AA-14

1. Yes
2. No
3. ?
4. No
5. Yes
6. b
7. d
8. a
9. c
10. c

AA-15

1. b
2. c
3. a
4. e
5. d
6. 4
7. 3
8. 1
9. 2
10. a

AA-16

1. Yes
2. No
3. ?
4. Yes
5. No
6. Yes
7. 2
8. 1
9. 4
10. 3
11. a. bus
12. b. car
13. c. girl
14. d. teacher
15. b

AA-17

1. Yes
2. No
3. ?
4. Yes
5. ?
6. d
7. b
8. a
9. c
10. b

AA-18

1. Yes
2. Yes
3. No
4. No
5. Yes
6. ?
7. a
   b
   c
   e
8. c
9. b
10. b

AA-19

1. Yes
2. No
3. ?
4. Yes
5. No
6. 2
7. 1
8. 4
9. 3
10. c

AA-20

1. Yes
2. No
3. ?
4. No
5. Yes
6. No
7. Yes
8. No
9. Yes
10. d
11. e
12. a
13. b
14. c
15. c

AA-21

1. No
2. ?
3. Yes
4. Yes
5. 4
6. 1
7. 5
8. 2
9. 3
10. a

AA-22

1. Yes
2. ?
3. Yes
4. No
5. Yes
6. ?
7. hospital
8. sign
9. cleaners
10. a

AA-23

1. Yes
2. ?
3. No
4. Yes
5. ?
6. 2
7. 4
8. 1
9. 5
10. 3
11. d
12. c
13. b
14. a
15. c

AA-24

1. Yes
2. No
3. ?
4. Yes
5. No
6. b
7. d
8. a
9. c
10. a

AA-25

1. Yes
2. ?
3. ?
4. No
5. No
6. children
7. window
8. shirt
9. hospital
10. c

AA-26

1. b
2. c
3. d
4. a
5. a
6. c
7. b
8. a
9. c
10. b

AA-27

1. Yes
2. No
3. No
4. ?
5. ✓ a.
   ___ b.
   ✓ c.
   ___ d.
   ___ e.
6. 3
7. 2
8. 1
9. 4
10. c

AA-28

1. Earth
2. time
3. 24 hours
4. 93,000,000 miles
5. 864,000 miles
6. fire
7. a
   c
   d
8. b
9. c
10. b

AA-29

1. a
2. b
3. b
4. a
5. a
6. b
7. b
8. a
   b
   d
   e
9. c
10. a

AA-30

1. Yes
2. Yes
3. No
4. Yes
5. No
6. Yes
7. b
8. c
9. a
10. "in"
11. children
12. older
13. light
14. a
15. c